YOUNG AT HEART

By
Fiona Young

YOUNG AT HEART

Author: Fiona Young

Copyright © 2025 Fiona Young

The right of Fiona Young to be identified as author of this work has been asserted by the author in accordance with section 77 and 78 of the Copyright, Designs and Patents Act 1988.

First Published in 2025

ISBN 978-1-83538-747-4 (Paperback)
978-1-83538-748-1 (Hardback)
978-1-83538-749-8 (E-Book)

Book Cover Design and Book Layout by:
White Magic Studios
www.whitemagicstudios.co.uk

Published by:
Maple Publishers
Fairbourne Drive, Atterbury,
Milton Keynes,
MK10 9RG, UK
www.maplepublishers.com

A CIP catalogue record for this title is available from the British Library.

All rights reserved. No part of this book may be reproduced or translated in any form or by any means, electronic or mechanical, including photocopying, recording or by any information storage and retrieval system without written permission from the author.

The views expressed in this work are solely those of the author and do not necessarily reflect the publisher's opinions, and the publisher, as a result of this, disclaims any responsibility for them.

CONTENTS

Prologue 5

Chapter 1.. 10

Chapter 2.. 27

Chapter 3.. 35

Chapter 4.. 42

Chapter 5.. 47

Chapter 6.. 50

Chapter 7.. 56

Chapter 8.. 64

Chapter 9.. 73

Chapter 10.. 77

This is a true story

To my wonderful daughters Scarlett and Aimee I love you to bits and my gorgeous grandkids Alfie, Mila, Lottie and Zoe

My Grandkids Alfie Mila Lottie and Zoe

Acknowledgements

Thanks to my nephew David for all his help with the production of this memoir!

Also thanks to **Maple Publishers** for being great!

Prologue

I'm clairvoyant. I've been told by the mediums but I've known since I was 40 when my beloved Dad died. He wasn't just my Dad but also my best friend. I loved spending time with him. He was so kind, funny, highly intelligent, full of great stories and intellectual things to say. He loved to get drunk. Gin and tonics and Guinness at lunch time then Famous Grouse whisky and water. We had great times getting drunk together. I'm the eldest of his 3 daughters and he never had a son so he took me to football matches, golf, cricket, pub crawling, sitting on barstools people watching and lots of gigs. We went to Frank Sinatra, Billy Connolly and the Stones to name a couple. Dad and Mum adored each other and their family more than words can say. They met when Dad was the up and coming accountant at a big engineering company in Cathcart, Glasgow. Mum was in charge of the punch card department ie Dad was the boss and she was the worker but they fell madly in love. Mum's best friend was emigrating to Canada and Mum was going to go so Dad said marry me and she said yes and they were married very quickly. Everyone thought it was a shotgun wedding but I didn't come along till 3 years later. Growing up with them was brill and the house was always full of laughter. Mum and Dad did things to make each other laugh and us all laugh. Holidays were in St Tropez and Juan Les Pins. My Dad couldn't see past the South of France. He was a creature of habit and he loved France (we all did) so he didn't see the point of going anywhere else. We did a few times and it was always a disaster. Instead to vary

France we would always go a different mode of transport. Sometimes flying, driving, the train and sometimes the car on the sleeper train. They also used to leave us with Granny and Mum's sister Auntie Diana and go on date weekends to the George V in Paris and the Cipriani in Venice. Like Michael Caine and Shakira.

    I felt my Dad the moment he died with massive goosebumps starting at my feet then engulfing my whole body up to my head. I was working in Manchester catering for a BBC drama called Common as Muck with a great cast who were so lovely to me. Kathy Burke was psychic too. She talked to me a lot about her Dad and she was so understanding. A lovely woman. Roy Hudd became my new Dad and Neil Dudgeon was great to me too. Anyway I had to fly to Glasgow to be with my family. On the plane I could see my Dad on a cloud with my beloved Uncle Russell who had died 3 years before. They were drinking their whiskies and people watching making their usual cheeky comments. I also passed my sis in law and great friend Lydia in the air. She was going to Manchester to take over running my job.

Me and Lydia

The family decided I should fly to London to get my youngest sister Kirsty off a plane from Greece and tell her about Dad. Mum didn't want us to phone her and her trying frantically to get home. More flying in the sky with my family on the clouds. On the plane I met José who was from Mexico and in Europe to see it before he settled down and got married. He was a guardian angel sent by my Dad. Obviously I was majorly in bits drinking my vodka and tonics on the plane and shouting 'Meet José' to the whole plane. Then he propelled me all round London spoon feeding me pasta in Kings Road and getting me to Victoria Station then on the Gatwick Express. We couldn't get a taxi to Victoria so José flagged one down with people in it and told them about me and my Dad. They said jump in no problem and we'll drop you at Victoria. Turned out they were an Irish rock band going to the recording studio. It was U2. I'm not good at recognising celebrities but my Dad told me later it was them. They exuded fame and they were all gorgeous looking. Definitely famous rock stars.

When we got to Gatwick José mysteriously disappeared and I got Kirsty off the plane. She knew it was about Dad as soon as she saw me there. We went for a vodka and tonic to toast Dad's wonderful life and José even more mysteriously reappeared to get us to Kirsty's flat, pack and fly up to Glasgow.

On the morning of Dad's funeral I woke up at 3am and went to my office in the house. I was still working on the film and tv catering business but I'd been rolling about crying on my lounge floor listening to loud jazz for days drinking loads of vodka and tonic and not sleeping so I knew I had to pay all my bills before I went to Dad's funeral to say goodbye and see you in the next life. So I got my notebook out and made a list of what I owed. I had a red pen and found myself viciously underlining the VAT and PAYE. Dad's priorities to get paid then I split the rest between all my suppliers the way Dad had taught me. The red pen underlined the VAT so much it made massive holes in the paper nearly through to the end of the pad. The power in my hand was so strong but everything must be paid before I went to the funeral which he was happy about.

I spent a few years going to clairvoyant seminars and workshops to learn about being a medium. I feel Dad all the time especially when I'm having a few drinks with friends and family talking about him and listening to his favourite jazz music. He gets me parking spaces too. It's his speciality. I say right Faa...ther I need a space and someone pulls out right in front of me.

In my meditation I have a white paddock with three beautiful horses in it. A black one, a bay and a white one. Dad has the bay, Uncle Russell the white and Johnny Cash the black. They are friends with him. I have always loved Johnny Cash but Dad was mainly big on his jazz. Louis Armstrong, Duke Ellington and Billy Holiday but he also liked lots of other music like Dusty Springfield and Kenneth McKellar. Anyway the three of them go out bareback riding on them. I don't know about Johnny Cash but Dad and Russell used to ride bareback on Earth. We are descended from gypsies. They visit all the spirits who are unhappy. Maybe having trouble connecting with their loved ones and they help them.

Dad was 71 when he died 29 years ago now but Mum lasted till 96 without him, enjoying her daughters, grandkids and great grandkids. Never another man would replace my Dad. Mum died peacefully in her sleep with no health issues on 3rd January this 2024 so I'm now talking to her. That will come later.

Mum at 90

Mum and her 3 daughters

Chapter 1

My earliest childhood memory is when I was 4. My sister Trish was a late speaker and we were in bed but not sleeping. Trish said 'Mum' and my Mum came in and gave me into trouble for talking when I was supposed to be sleeping. I said no Mum it was Trish but my Mum didn't believe me.

Our childhood in Newton Mearns Glasgow was truly amazing. There was always so much laughter in the house. Dad would make Mum laugh and she would make him laugh. They always did silly quirky things to make each other laugh then us kids would laugh too. There was so much love.

Humbie Road

We moved to Humbie Road. Mum and Dad bought the land and built the house to their own design to suit the needs of them and their 2 girls. The hall had a 40 foot clear glass window with views of the garden. Mum made the curtains. How she managed such large curtains I don't know but she was great at sewing. She made all her clothes. Evening dresses so when she went to business do's with Dad she wouldn't be wearing the same dress as someone else. She made our clothes too even our bikinis. The kitchen was huge and amazing for her fab cooking. There was open shelving to our big playroom with her favourite plants so she could watch us to make sure we were playing safely. In the playroom there were big cupboards for our toys that we could climb on top of and a stage with curtains the full length of the room where we could do our shows and a wee stage for us to play with our large collection of puppets. Next to the playroom was a toilet for us. The living room was huge with circular couches and a black and white tv. It was L shaped where the dining table was. We also had a cosy snug. There was a door from the playroom into the back garden where they built a 10 foot concrete sandpit which we played in all the time. Trish split here head on the concrete once but she was fine. The gate at the bottom of the garden led to a field. We could run up the hill and across the next field to a café to get our sweets and ice creams. The neighbours had ponies in their field which we learnt to ride. Our Aunt Diana used to ski down the hill. Mum planted the whole garden with amazing plants and shrubs. It's incredible how the garden looks now with all the mature planting that's just colossal.

My cousin Graeme came to stay with us for a while when his Mum was in hospital. He was the older brother I never had and I loved him to bits. He was so good looking. I was 10 and he was 14. He used to sneak into my bedroom at night to look at me through my see through nightie. We played in the quarry across the road. In the field at the quarry we put paper bags over the burrows to try to catch the rabbits with no success. We used to sit on a rock at the top of the quarry and look down at the water there. There was a bush at the back of the ledge that we hid in and bared our bums to each other. What you do at that age! In the winter the water was frozen and we could skate on it.

Graeme was a bit of a lad. At Christmas he woke us all up at 2 in the morning firing his gun. Then he was sitting behind the curtains in the hall with the sun on his magnifying glass and burnt holes in my Mum's beautiful curtains. She fixed them. He also loved pulling apart a golf ball.

Our neighbours across the road had a peacock and down the road they had a goose which bit me on the ankle once. It was a huge hole that took ages to heal.

It was about this time that Uncle John returned from the Merchant Navy travelling the world. He was sporting a horrid orange beard which made us all laugh.

In those days children got buses by themselves so Mum and Dad would send us off to the bus stop in Newton Mearns to go and stay with our Granny and Auntie Diana who lived in a one bed tenement flat at Eglinton Toll next to the railway line. Granny or Diana would get us off the bus. There was no bathroom but we loved having a bath in the kitchen sink or in a basin in front of the fire. We used to play in the back yard in the mud. My Mum did that when she was a child. Granny would throw pieces and jam down to us from the 2nd floor. What fun for kids. She would do that too when she came to our house. She would throw them from the kitchen window to our sandpit in the garden.

When I was 11 we moved to Wolverhampton. Dad had changed his job to an engineering company called J Walter Thomsons because he had been doing too much travelling with his previous job at Weirs in Glasgow and he missed us all so much. Anyway this job was less travelling but when he did travel it was to Australia and the Far East instead of Europe and he had to stay 3 weeks at a time. We hated it when he was away that long and we put his picture on his favourite armchair.

We lived in a flat until they found us a house. I made friends with a lovely 17 year old girl called Marianne across the road. She wore floral mini dresses and Dr Scholl sandals with bare feet. It was the 60s and that was the fashion. I was in awe of her she was so beautiful with long blonde hair. She bought The Beatles Sgt. Peppers LP when it came out and she played it for me. I loved it. It was an amazing album. I liked The Beatles, The Monkees and Cilla Black at that time. I bought the singles with my pocket money. My first single was Cilla Black Anyone Who Has A Heart and my next one was The Beatles All You Need Is Love and I'm A Believer by The Monkeys. I used to record them on my tape cassette machine, rewind and write down each line. That was how I learnt the words so I could sing along. I still remember the words to these songs today.

So there was a building site opposite our flat where they were laying the foundations for more flats. There were bricks and building materials everywhere so we built a wee house. Another den. We had a wee fire. Acceptable in those days. Mum loved it and she brought us picnics there. The builders didn't mind we weren't doing any harm and they had kids of their own so they knew how much fun we were having. Marianne would come in the den and play guitar and sing Beatles songs to us.

Me at Rumford

Rumford and the woods

Rumford on the terrace

Rumford

Then we moved into the house in the country in Staffordshire. We lived at Rumford which was Mum and Dad's dream house. A fabulous mansion in the heart of the country with 9 acres of woods and 2 fields between us and the neighbours. It had a courtyard where I taught myself to drive in Mum's pale blue Austin (a very funny bubble car) going round and round it. The cleaner and the gardener lived in a house at the bottom of the driveway. The garden was amazing. It had a huge raised lawn with a weeping willow tree. We would go inside it and make a den in it. We could also go in the rhododendrons. They were huge and we made dens in them too. We would get pheasants and rabbits on the lawn. The gardener would shoot the pheasants and hang them in the garage. Then Mum would cook them for Dad's dinner. I loved being in the woods. I climbed the trees. I could go very high up and look down on the daffodils that covered the paths through the woods. I collected the leaves from the trees. Then I would look them up in my wee Readers Digest book of trees that Dad had bought me, put them in a scrapbook and write the name of the tree on them. I also caught butterflies on our lawn with a net and made a picture from them. We got hundreds of butterflies in our garden.

I was a terrible teenager I was covered in acne on my face chest and back for a while which made me miserable and I couldn't go out to the youth clubs and meet boys. Then the doctor said I may have a hormone imbalance and put me on the pill. The acne went away and I was able to go out and socialise again.

I was horrible to Mum when I had the acne. She would chase me round the garden with a slipper or a riding crop but I would climb a big tree and laugh at her from up there where she couldn't reach me. When my Dad came home from work at the weekends. He travelled the world with his job but he was always home for his family at the weekends. He loved his family life so much. So he would say I want to talk to you what's wrong. I was putty with my Dad and always did what he told me so I would say nothing I'm fine and he would say that ok then and give me a big hug.

There was a huge stone terrace at the back of the house. I used to walk back and forward on the terrace when I was doing homework or learning for exams. I would read out loud and remember what I'd read the next day at school. I had a photographic memory then so I could remember what I'd read word for word the next day so I passed all my exams and I was top of my class at school.

I remember one time the skinhead gang came to our house. I used to go to the village nearby Kinver and hang out. There was a skinhead gang there. They went on their scooters with knives to the neighbouring villages to fight the other gangs. I loved the leader of the gang Josh. He was my first love but he was a rogue. He looked like James Dean. He was gorgeous. Faded jeans, a pink shirt and red braces with bovver boots and a leather jacket. My parents were away on a date weekend and they left us in the house so I invited the gang to come round for drinks much to the horror of my sister Trish. They arrived and I panicked and locked all the doors but they shimmied up the drainpipes and came in my bedroom window. The gardener's wife our cleaner had seen the van arriving and Mum must have told her to keep an eye on us because she came to the door to check everything was ok. I told her not to worry it was all fine. They were my friends. So as you can imagine they found my Dad's drinks cupboard in the sideboard in the dining room and they drank all the booze. He had loads of fags in there too so they smoked them all. We did manage to get them to go eventually and there was no damage to our lovely house. Dad found it funny that we'd had a party and drunk all his booze and smoked all his fags. He had a good laugh at it. He was expecting the house to be trashed.

There was another night when I was at a youth club full of all the skinhead gangs from the area. I was with my friend Julie Heathcock from school. I was dancing with a guy called Flea, another leader of another gang, and while we were dancing I felt a huge knife in his pocket. I panicked and called my Mum from the phone box (Dad was abroad). She came with Julie's mother Beryl with sticks and dogs to fend off the enemy but by the time they got there the skinhead gangs had gone off on their scooters probably to do more fighting in the villages.

Next door 2 fields away was Roy Wood from the band The Move. He had a pink Cadilac that he used to drive at high speeds on the country roads. We were in the garage once and he was there. Much to our horror Mum decided to go and introduce herself and complain about his driving.

A year later my sister Kirsty was born on Christmas Eve. She was 2 weeks early so Mum wasn't prepared for Christmas and she was in hospital. Dad tried to cook for us. Mum did everything for him so he couldn't cook. We've never forgotten the black mince he made us. Then on Christmas Eve we could hear him doing Santa in their bedroom through the wall from us. All we could hear was FUCK FUCK FUCK as he tried to sort out who was getting what presents. On Christmas Day he took us out to a restaurant. We were miserable. Our Christmas Days were always so lovely and festive with all the family coming from Glasgow and London.

We were 2 miles from the nearest bus stop. Trish and I were teenagers and we wanted to go to youth clubs. My Dad wouldn't let Mum take us out at night so he would take us and that interfered with the whiskies he enjoyed after a hard day at the office.

They had to give up their dream house and we moved to a town called Stourbridge across the road from a bus stop. At least it got me away from the skinheads but I was throwing tantrums galore about my 'boyfriend' Josh so Dad said he would take me to see him. I said no because he was horrible to me and he had another girlfriend. Also I didn't want Dad to meet the skinhead gang. We soon made new friends a much nicer crowd so I forgot about the skinheads. We went to a lovely guy Rick Sherrat's house a lot to smoke weed and listen to Neil Young's latest album. Rick wanted to marry me. He was very handsome but he was too nice for me. I liked the bad boys. My sister's friend Lesley from school still knows him and he hasn't aged well apparently. Very fat and bald!

Stourbridge

Stourbridge

This house was lovely too. I remember the beautiful yellow roses everywhere and trellises of plants and flowers. Mum was a great gardener so the garden was amazing.

Trellises at Stourbridge

We got invited to our neighbour's pool party but Trish and I didn't want to go to an oldies party. Mum came rushing across to get us because a famous radio DJ was there. We told her to get lost.

We used to go to an arts club in Stourbridge called The Mere. Bands who lived locally would come and play there. We saw Led Zepplin and Marmalade. We used to steal apples from John Bonham's Aunts garden.

One night I was out with Julie in another club in Stourbridge. I was staying over at Julie's. I loved staying there because she had an older brother John who had lots of friends potential boyfriends for me. John was gorgeous too he had red curly hair. So I got offered a lift home by some guys but Julie waited for her Mum to pick her up. They were all drunk including the driver and as he sped round a roundabout the car turned over. We all got out uninjured but I was scared and shaken so I ran off. An older man in a car saw me and stopped and offered me a lift home to Julie's so I took it. My white tights were all ripped from the crash so he said he had spare pairs in the boot. This seemed very strange and I was terrified but I knew I needed to get home to Julie's. It turned out he was a salesman and they were his stock so I got home safely and Julie's mum brought me tea in bed in the morning like she always did.

I went to school at Holy Trinity Convent in Kidderminster where they make carpets. The school was stunning and brand new. It had a massive all wood and glass hallway with a huge spiral staircase where we had assembly. Open plan wooden floors to all the classrooms. There was an Olympic size swimming pool in a glass room and a hockey pitch and netball courts outside. One day at hockey a girl in my class fainted. She had an abortion. It was run by nuns who lived in the quarters next to the school. Nuns are supposed to live in poverty but these ones didn't. I sneaked in one day and they had fabulous accommodation all wood panelling like the school with fitted wardrobes and wooden beds. The school was a mixture of catholic and non catholic kids. Us non catholics paid fees but the Catholic girls didn't. We were told they wouldn't force religion on us but we were made to go to chapel every Friday and do the rosary. Then one of the nuns died and the whole school had to file past her open coffin. I will always remember that yellow nun. It was horrible for a child. Whenever one of the nuns had a feast day we all had to bring flowers. Mum picked a beautiful bunch of flowers from her garden. The plant was Mum's pride and joy and she hated picking from it. She liked to look at it in its glory in her beautiful garden. Trish saw them in the bin and she was very upset. As if they couldn't have taken them to the nearest hospital or childrens home if they didn't want them. The nuns were very hypocritical.

I was permanently being sent out of class for talking and passing notes. I spent most of my school years in amongst the coats but I still managed to come top of the class every time I was so clever. Sometimes I would be sent to the headmistress's office. She was a very small wizened nun called Sister Marie Rose and she was evil. She used to beat me up with the ruler on the back of my hand. It was so sore I will never forget it. The Reverend Mother was lovely though. One time in Miss George's biology class we were doing what happens to a ham sandwich in the body when you eat it. I was talking all the way through so she asked me to come to the front of the class and tell the story. I told it as she had said it. I could listen and talk at the same time so I remembered it word for word. She was livid so she told me I was a bad influence on my friend Julie who wasn't very clever and sent me out the class.

I made a beautiful blue dress at my sewing class. It was low cut at the front and backless so you could see all my acne. The sewing teacher gave me the first prize and wanted me to show it off at a fashion show for the parents where we came down the spiral stairs in the assembly hall. I threw a tantrum because I couldn't have everyone seeing my acne and I refused to do it. The teacher was livid. I was very good at sewing and her star pupil.

We all left school at 16 which was as soon as we could. School was so horrible. I went to Bromsgrove College of Further Education to do my A levels. It was a 2 year course and I loved the freedom of being at college and living a life. I hitchhiked to college every day and kept my bus fare for booze and fags in the common room. 10 Sovereign were 10p in those days. Everybody hitchhiked everywhere. I would usually get picked up by Clifford T Ward a famous singer songwriter of the day. He had a Scimitar which was a very posh car then. He worked as a teacher at the school next door to my college. He was a lovely guy and a great singer. He had lots of hit records. The common room was fab lots of guys with guitars. I loved it at college.

I left one very wet morning to get the bus to Stourbridge and get a job. I trawled round every shop and café with lots of no's but I didn't give up. I was determined to get a job and earn some money that I wouldn't stop till I got one that wet day. I got a job in Woolworths. I was on the pick and mix counter and was permanently on the floor eating the sweets. One day I was doing stocktaking in the storeroom and a box of shampoo fell on my head. I didn't hurt myself but my hair was covered in loads of shampoo. I went to the ladies to wash it out but there was so much of it the bubbles covered the whole toilet floor and out the door. I got the sack.

My next job was great at a pub called the Foley Arms across the road from our house. I was only 16 but I was allowed to make Irish coffees. That's coffee cream and Jamesons Irish whisky. I learned to float the cream and for years after I was making my Dad his favourite Irish coffees floating the cream beautifully for him.

There were various boyfriends at this time. The first one had a big red sports car but he was too nice for me so I picked Steve Coldicott a fabulous looking rogue with no car but he had a flat and he played the guitar. I went to meet him at Tiffanys night club in Halesowen and he stood me up so I drank several brandies and babysham and felt sick. I couldn't be sick in the toilets they were full of sick it was discusting so I ran to the back of the car park and was sick in the bushes.

Martin Stallard a surfing dood was my next boyfriend. I thought he was gorgeous but the family thought he was a joke. He travelled the world following the surf to Biarritz, Hawaii and Australia. We had a den in our house. It was an integral garage converted for us by Mum as a party room for us to bring our boyfriends. We had a stereo and a tv in there and comfy couches. Big posters on the wall of my favourite naked Cat Stevens, David Cassidy and The Monkees. Trish had Deep Purple, Black Sabbath and TRex. It was great. There was a back door but Mum and Dad insisted they came in the front door and through the kitchen so they could be vetted by my Dad, Uncle Russell and Cousin Graeme who were sitting at the kitchen table drinking their whiskies. Mum was cooking, They would howl with laughter at my latest man. He had feathered hair like the band The Sweet very tall because he was wearing 6 inch platform silver lamy boots and a tight leather jacket. They were laughing loudly right in front of him. It's hilarious thinking back.

Uncle Russell

Then came the devastating news for me we were moving back to Glasgow.

So I had to leave Martin Stallard the love of my life and move back to Glasgow.

I was 17 and learning to drive. I had a few lessons but mainly Mum and Dad taught me on the country roads. Remember I started driving at Rumford in the courtyard when I was 14 so I thought I could already drive but little did I know it wasn't as easy as first gear round a courtyard. Anyway Mum had a rickety old Avenger. Mum and Dad had plenty of money but Dad wouldn't spend it on cars it was a waste so he bought Mum old bangers. He had his company cars. Jaguars and Daimlers. So I am belting along the country roads and Mum is permanently pulling on the handbrake and screaming at me to slow down. On the night before my test I was practising reversing in the driveway. I reversed into the carport and took the drainpipe with me. Dad said it was like falling off a horse you had to get back on so he took me out driving straight away. I got a cancellation because we were leaving the country and I passed my test first time but I couldn't drive so I don't know how I passed. I was driving to college the next day to say bye to all my college friends and lecturers and I had a very scary time at a big motorway roundabout. I don't know to this day how I survived it I was so scared of all the traffic and massive lorries speeding round the roundabout.

I was wailing in the car all the way to Glasgow. Trish remembers it vividly to this day and still talks about it. Me, Trish and Kirsty were all with Mum and the budgie Timmy was on my knee. We stopped overnight at The Tickled Trout in Preston. We found out later it was a famous haunt for cheating couples but I didn't see any I was too busy crying over leaving Martin.

Chapter 2

So we arrive back in Glasgow and we move into Milverton Road Giffnock. A lovely area on the south side of Glasgow. Mum and Dad always get their houses the way they want them and they do a lot of the work themselves so my Mum is in a boiler suit with a sledgehammer knocking down walls . Dads priority is his jazz music so he is wiring every room with speakers. He is too big to go under the floorboards so Mum who is small does that and he pokes the wires through to her.

Dad hates to see me upset and I am still crying about leaving Martin so Dad says he can come anytime he wants. He is thinking that I will soon meet new friends and a new boyfriend but Martin arrives the next day. He hitchhiked up. The house is a building site. Piles of rubble and my bed is in the middle of the lounge surrounded by bricks and tea chests. There is nowhere for Martin to sleep but Mum being Mum soon rustles up a bed for him. Can you imagine what a nightmare that was for my parents but their priority was to keep me happy.

I went down to Birmingham on the overnight bus often. Martin and his Dad picked me up from the bus station in a fire engine. His dad was a fireman. What fun that was and he put on the siren so we jumped the lights.

My Granny , Mum's Mum, would visit us all the time. She was great and I loved her to bits. She used to have auburn hair down past her waist with a silver streak through it (my daughter has that now). Then she had her hair cut and it was thick and wild. She always wore a pinnie (apron) even at our house. She would put her fag ends in the pocket. She would walk the length of Victoria Road looking for the cheapest fags. On the way she would go to Curleys grocers and buy us fresh butter from a big block that they took lumps off with a paddle and put it on the greaseproof paper. It was delicious. I loved her reading my tea leaves. She did it for her whole neighbourhood.

I was at Langside College to finish my A levels and as Dad thought I quickly made new friends and forgot about Martin. My best friend was Gillian Maxwell. I fancied the English teacher who was called Norman so I stickered his name on the front of my orange Mini. The rest of it was covered in Snoopy stickers.

Dad then set about finding a social life for us and Uncle John had said Joanna's nightclub was a good night on a Monday. You got tickets for it in a pub called the Griffin across the road. Me, Trish, Mum and Dad set off for the Griffin and Dad walked all round the bar trying to get tickets for us. No luck so we had to leave. I was wailing again as usual. Anyway at the door a guy came up and offered us tickets so it was happy ever after.

Gillian and I used to go the Glasgow University Womens Union every Saturday. There was live music on there. We sat in the bar but we could hear the music and when anyone good came on we would go downstairs to watch. One night in 1971 the music was amazing so we rushed down as quick as we could. The lead singer was gorgeous in a gold lamy suit and they blew us away. He was Freddie Mercury and it was Queen starting out. What a concert I will never forget it.

My cousin Graeme would come up from London every New Year. It's so good in Glasgow . We would go to parties. I had such fun with him. We'd hide behind a pillar and he would tell me which boys were looking at me and I would tell him which girls were sussing him. The Jewish princesses all fancied him he was drop dead gorgeous with long tousled hair and his John Mayall jacket on. The Jewish men were not amused. One night a very good looking guy was looking at me and he came over and invited me to a dinner dance. Tuns out he was a professional footballer playing for Dumbarton and this was the club dinner. How exciting. My friend Gillian fancied him so she fell out with me and never spoke to me again. Anyway Tom McAdam ended up playing for Celtic and we had a lovely time together. He was wealthy and we used to walk across the field from his flat in Scotstoun to the Pond Hotel on Great Western Road for dinners. He had won a Ford Capri in the Rangers Pools. It was yellow with black slats. Everyone's dream car at the time. Anyway he couldn't drive so his brother used it but we would sit in it in the carpark play music and chat. It all sounds idyllic but unfortunately he was too nice for me so I dumped him.

My sister was at Craigholme School and she got into a very nice crowd of girls who were seeing some really nice boys. She would bring them all round to Milverton Road where we had another den garage conversion in the basement. There were stairs down from the hall, a toilet and a door from our back garden but for some reason everyone used to come in through the window on the driveway. I really don't know why they didn't use the door. Maybe it was more exciting. I was there and soon got in with this crowd. I was seeing a guy with a purple fiberglass sports car and one of the guys burnt a hole in it jealous .

We were starting to have a great social life. Everyone went to the same discos every week. The Redhurst on a Sunday was fab and local. It was great for meeting people when you went to the same places.

I had such fun in my wee Mini pub crawling with the friends with bottles all over the floor. I got stopped by the police once for going down a one way street the wrong way but they didn't notice the bottles and they said I had a kind face so they let me go.

I had a job in the McDonald Hotel across the road from our house. I worked in the lounge bar but I was good so they moved me round the bars. Sometime the public bar where the guys would ask me for a hauf and a hauf. I hadn't a clue what that was at first but I soon learned it was a whisky and a half pint of beer. I was also in the cocktail bar which was very posh and I did some functions which were lovely with everyone all dressed up.

So I got my A Levels and I went to Glasgow College of Technology to do a bilingual secretarial course with French. By then I was fluent in French. I'd spent all my family holidays there and I had a Higher and an A Level. The course was great except the shorthand. I couldn't get the hang of all those squiggles and it seemed unnecessary to me. Why couldn't you just write part of a word then make sense of it in the context of the sentence. So I passed all the course except the shorthand. Turns out I would never need it in life anyway. I wanted to work in Paris, I love Paris, and in advertising, tourism or fashion. Part of the course was a placement which had to be France. I obviously chose the South and I set about trying to find a job. I wrote to all the big fancy hotels in Cannes. Most of them sent polite replies but no vacancies. I was going on my own but Paul my friend from Langside had a girlfriend called Dorothy. I didn't know her but he said she would love to go to France. We went together and I soon got to know her. She was a lovely girl and looked like a Barbie doll. Blonde hair and porcelain skin. We went student travel and it cost us £20 for the journey by trains and ferry. We didn't have a sleeper for the train in the UK and through France but we shut the door, pulled down the blinds and went to sleep on the bench seats. Nobody disturbed us. We woke up in St Rafael and it was a glorious day. We were in the South of France. One of the best places in the World.

Me France

We found a hotel up a back street for £2 a night in Juan Les Pins where I'd always gone with my family and we lived on bread, cheese and fruit. We would go out in the evening to the Crystal Café. It was such a buzzing lively café full of interesting, good looking people. We allowed ourselves 5 francs for a Chocolate Legioux or a Campari and Soda. I took my 5 francs to the casino across the road and bet my lucky numbers 5 and 6 on roulette. I always won (I'm very lucky) so we had the ice cream and the drink. During the day we trolled all the hotels looking for work with no luck. We went to agencies too. One night we came home to the hotel and there was a note on the door from Dad. I'm in Le Provencal come and see me. This was the best hotel in Juan Les Pins. It was fabulous. Dad gave us money and dinner. He wanted me to do this myself but he couldn't resist helping a little bit. He had been working in Milan and he took the 20 min flight to Nice to see me and check I was ok. Dad did that a few times and it was great to keep me going. My family also came for their 2 week holiday so we moved into their apartment and did all the cleaning and shopping for our keep.

Eventually we got great jobs as chambermaids in a beautiful exclusive hotel in La Garoupe which is between Juan Les Pins and Antibes. It has a lovely beach. This hotel was mainly people who were travelling round the area so they had big cars and were all very wealthy. We had to work very hard. The French have very high standards of cleanlieness. They wash the pavements outside the cafes and restaurants every morning. So every day we changed the beds and towels washed under the beds and all the windows. It was bed and breakfast only so we served petit dejeuner on a tray to the balconies. I had a lot of fun speaking French to people like the Goldbergs from London then listening to them talking about me in English thinking I couldn't understand. There was a very rich very fat woman with a wee dog who stayed the whole summer. All the French women have wee dogs. She had grapefruit every morning for breakfast but her wardrobes were full of cakes and sweets. She had a huge collection of Christian Dior make up and nail polishes. We tried them all on. We worked from 7 in the morning till 3 in the afternoon so after work we went to the beach and lay on luxurious padded sunbeds.

We were earning a lot on money so we got a nice studio flat in Antibes. We were washing the windows one day when some friends from Glasgow turned up in a fiat to visit. It was Paul Dorothy's boyfriend, Jim, Paul McLintock and Frank. They had no money to stay anywhere so we put them up in our flat and bought some lilos. This didn't go well with the French neighbours who were calling us putains (prostitutes) but we didn't care we were having fun with the boys. They hired mopeds and set off for the brilliant nightlife in Juan les Pins. They were on the beach every day but Jim remained white keeping his jeans and long sleeved shirt on and Frank wore socks with his swimming trunks. Weird but we had some fun times. Unfortunately Paul Mclintock was driving the car drunk and smashed it into the wall on the coast road. Nobody was hurt but the car was a write off so they had to get their parents to fly them home.

We were due to work until October but by September we had earned lots of money so we decided we deserved a holiday. We told the hotel a relative was sick and we left on good terms. The owners were lovely people. They gave us all this French National Insurance money so we had plenty for a month's holiday and we got a luxury studio in central Juan Les Pins. We went to the Crystal Cafe every night everyone went there. The guys would circle the café in their amazing cars checking out the girls in the café. It was just great. We saw Mick Jagger fall out of a car there one night.

We met some very rich guys from Richmond who were sleeping in the big pipes on the beach. We moved them into our studio. One of them had a Porsche beach buggy. It was huge. Another had a Harley Davidson. Dorothy's was the one with the buggy and mine the bike. He was called Michael and he looked like Michael Hutchence. We had such fun with them hairing along the roads and the beach in the buggy with us all hanging out the back. We had parties with a camp fire on the beach and we were permanently lighting up the Crystal Cafe. I was on the back of the bike in my bikini going along the coast road sideways round the bends with my knee on the road. We had the best time ever. Then their holiday was over. We had two weeks left but they invited us to Richmond on our way back to Glasgow. Dorothy had a great time but Michael had a girlfriend so I was just a fling but what a fling.

Chapter 3

Back to Glasgow and time to find a proper job. I was 19. I found one in an advertising agency as a receptionist. I called them at 8 in the morning and a lovely guy called Ian Skillen told me I was over qualified for the job but I wanted to work in advertising so I pleaded with him to give me the job. I got it but they soon realised my potential and they moved me around the departments till I ended up as an Account Manager looking after the clients. It was a great job with lovely people and I made some life long friends.

We used to go to Maestros night club every Saturday night. It wasn't licensed but we bought cokes and sneaked in the vodka in our handbags and filled up our glasses in the toilets. A David Cassidy look alike in a white suit asked me to dance one night. I loved David Cassidy. I watched him and the Partridge family on tv and I had a big poster of him in our den. We were dancing away when suddenly this girl came up to me and punched me on the face. Turned out he was supposed to be her boyfriend. I obviously punched her back and we got thrown out of Maestros and barred. This lovely girl Claire came to my rescue. She said she knew the owner because she worked in his hairdressers and she would take me to meet him and sort this out. I was devastated Maestros was a great club and everyone went there. The next day she took me to Clouds another night club and she explained what had happened to the owner. He realised it wasn't my fault and he said I could go back to Maestros. Claire became one of my best friends and has remained a good friend for life.

My sister Trish, me and a friend went to Newquay for a holiday. We went by coach and it took 2 days. One night I came home to the B+B to get an early night. I woke up in the morning to find a bunch of Plymouth CID in my room. A guy had apparently stabbed someone at the end of the road and ran away coming through my room and escaping out my window at the back of the building. I'm a sound sleeper and I didn't hear a thing.

By now I was 20 and it was in the lounge bar of the McDonald Hotel where I met Guy. I fancied him and I thought he was the tall dark handsome man my Granny had seen in my tea leaves years before. Turns out he was small but wearing 6 inch platform stars and striped boots with bell bottom jeans which hid the platforms. All the fashion at the time. It was 1976.

We went on a date and we were meant to be going to Edinburgh with the gang but Guy was late and we missed the train. Little did I know then that he was always going to be late. Anyway we went to the Redhurst Hotel on our own and we got on famously. He was intelligent, cheeky and witty with a good sense of humour and a lovable rogue. Just my type. I'd met my match.

We had great fun the next few years. Going out alone or with the pals. Drives to Ayr beach and barbecues on the sand. We had lots of dinners out with my family and Guy's. His Mum Bunty was brilliant. She sat at the top of the table and directed operations. Guy's two brothers and his three sisters were all outspoken and very witty. They all bounced off each other and the banter was great. Very funny dinners. A favourite haunt was the Marine Hotel in Troon. We also went with our best friends to Dumfries a lot, Guy went to boarding school there, and we stayed in a lovely place called Castle Douglas. Brunos restaurant in Dumfries was fab.

We saw Bob Marley and the Wailers at the Glasgow Apollo. It was fabulous the whole place was jumping. We also saw Kid Creole and the Coconuts there and we danced the night away.

We weren't allowed to live together in those days but we had sleep overs at each others houses when the parents were away. One morning Bunty came home and cleverly asked me and Guy in separate rooms where we had slept that night. By some strange fluke we got it right and she was happy.

We got engaged but I took cold feet and wasn't sure if I was ready to get married. My Granny the wise old woman who read the tea leaves loved Guy and persuaded me it was the right thing to do. Her words were always good enough for me. I adored my Granny.

All the presents started to come in and the stress got too much for me. Guy's Mum and Aunts were good Catholics and wanted the Church wedding but myself and my family were non religious and I wanted the registry office. I remember going round the roundabout at Clarkston Toll and throwing two lamps that were presents out of the car window. We safely retrieved them and we both decided on the registry office. Bunty and the Aunts were happy in the end.

I was very specific with the registrar that I didn't want to walk down an aisle. It was too religious for me. I also didn't want a white dress so I wore a lovely blue suit. My favourite colour. But they didn't heed my wishes and on the day they said I had to walk from a door at the back of the room to the front with my Dad. I just wanted to be sitting down and get up and get married. They told me this in the room I was waiting in with Dad. I threw a tantrum and poor Dad who had stopped smoking had to have one of my fags.

Anyway I got my wishes and the wedding was beautiful. The pictures were all in the lovely Eastwood Park and then we went across the road to Mum and Dad's house on Lynton Avenue for the reception. It was a huge white bungalow with an enormous garden that Mum had worked her magic on. There were fabulous Rhododendrons all the way up the driveway and at the front of the house. The hall was big and circular with all the rooms off it. Dad had taken all the doors off. We had the bar in the hall so people milled about there and the food on the large dining room table. Mum the great cook that she was had done a fantastic spread. The pianist from the Central Hotel was in the lounge. One of my Dad's favourite eating places and his favourite pianist.

Me and Dad at Lynton Avenue

My wedding

Me and Mum at my wedding

Aimee and Kyle

But my cousin Graeme my big brother hadn't arrived. He turned up late but I was so relieved I forgave him and he was looking wonderful in his dickie bow with a huge plant in a lovely white tiered pot.

Graeme and Trish at my wedding

When we left all the guys formed a row across the road and bared their bums. We had a night at the airport and 4 days in Amsterdam for our honeymoon where I saw my fav Van Goughs.

Chapter 4

I had several very enjoyable years at R + W Advertising then they merged with a big PR company called Charles Barker. They did PR for the Glasgow Marathon and several other prestigious clients. I didn't like PR it was boring compared to advertising so I decided to look for a new job. I got one as Account Manager with MCS based in an amazing big country house in Croftamie outside Drymen. Everyone had to get to the office miles out in the country so those of us with company cars picked people up at the beginning of the country road.

I had a great job there which was mainly recruitment advertising. There was big money to be made on national campaigns in the Times ,Telegraph and Financial Times. These national newspapers were very expensive and our commission was high. Silicone valley was formed in Scotland and all the big electronics companies were recruiting electronics engineers from the UK and abroad so advertising for them nationally and internationally. They were crying out for them so we were very busy. I loved this job and I worked for a lovely guy called Alan. He sent me off around Scotland to talk to all the electronic companies and persuade them to come together and do big ads featuring all of them because they were all looking for the same people.

We had some fab parties in the country house. Adjoining it was a conference centre with bedrooms so we all got to stay the night after the parties. Advertising was a very sociable industry and everyone partied.

Unfortunately the guy that owned the company had a quality car dealership which was in trouble so he syphoned off all the money the advertising agency was making and sunk it into his classic cars business. So we went bust.

We were swiftly taken over by the Rex Stewart Group and we formed Riley Advertising taking all our clients with us and gaining several from Rex Stewart. We had some great times. In those days entertaining the clients was a major part of the job so we took all our clients out on a Friday. Basically it was a piss up that lasted the whole afternoon and into the evening but we had the clients with us so it was classed as work. It wouldn't happen nowadays. We had to come in on Saturday mornings to make up the work we'd missed on Fridays but we didn't mind we had some fab times. I had my first claim to fame there. My boss was on holiday and I was asked to do a campaign called Life for Lanarkshire. Lots of jobs with the Lanarkshire Councils. My Dad was born and brought up in Motherwell, Lanarkshire so it was close to my heart. I won a major award for my ads. The Daily Express Recruitment Advertising Awards. I was presented with the award by David Jacobs at the Savoy in London and I got a trophy,

It was around this time that my beloved Granny died. To take my mind off it I went to Lindos on Rhodes with my good friend Claire. She was so funny and really cheered me up. She got badly bitten by the mosquitos. They didn't like me but they loved her and she was covered in huge red swollen bites. She insisted I didn't wear perfume which attracted them. Lindos is beautiful no cars just narrow winding cobbled streets and donkeys that took you up the hill to the monument. We were staying with a Greek family in a lovely house with a stone flowery courtyard. In Greece you have to put your toilet paper in a bin and not down the toilets because the drainage wasn't good enough.

I met a Zorba dancer called George who performed every night in the local taverna where they smashed the plates. It was brill. He was an amazing dancer. He had such strong arms and legs and he hung from the light fittings in the ceiling as part of his dance. We went to the disco after he finished work and we danced to Billy Jean by Michael Jackson. He used to throw me in the air then run at top speed to the other end of the dancefloor and catch me. Me being the daredevil that I was loved it. We had such fun there. We went back the following year but my friend George had gone to work in the main town so we didn't see him again.

Guys family grocers business had folded. He didn't know what to do so he spoke to my Mum and she said what would you like to do. He said he would love to have a shop with hanging salamis so my Mum said well go for it and I will help you. My Dad did his books.

Mum was fitting out the shop for him. She had done loads of big houses so a shop was an easy job for her. The tiles she picked for the walls were pale blue, pale green, lemon and pink inspired by my stripey swimsuit in the same colours. The glass fridges were the full length of the shop. There were beautiful hanging white globe lights with Guy's in black on them. It was called Guy's Delicatessen. Mum was working with Joe the Joiner. Mum's attention to detail was tremendous. She had measured the tins so that 3 fitted neatly on each shelf. Joe the joiner was doing his own thing but Mum swiftly insisted he do it her way. He soon realised he couldn't mess with Mum.

So Guy had his wish a beautiful deli with his hanging meats which looked great against the colourful tiles and mirrors. A huge selection of cheeses and meats in the cabinets, salads and cakes made by Mum.

The shop was a big success. Byres Road was central West End and loads of people flocked there. We bought a lovely sandstone conversion in Athole Gardens just off Byres Road and a 5 minute walk to the shop.

Me Athole Gardens

Guy needed my help to save wages starting out and Scarlett was a baby so I made the decision to leave my job in advertising and help him with the business. I used to walk to my work with the pram and our two dogs. Scarlett was a great baby so she sat in the pram playing with her toys while I worked the till. Happy in the bright coloured shop with all the people talking to her. The dogs were tied up out the back.

I drove our big yellow van to the fruit market every day to get the supplies. It was great fun there. The banter from all the guys was hilarious. We had some great parties with my advertising friends in that van.

Darlinda a famous Scottish clairvoyant used to come into the shop all the time. She lived in West end. I could feel her reading my mind. I saw her at a Publicity Club once. She was the speaker and she was phenomenal. She said I had a huge aura.

A few years later the Council shut all the shops to reroof the building. We were shut for a year and the competition had opened up round the corner and taken all our customers. We couldn't make it work then. We eventually got compensation from the Council but it was too late and the shop went into liquidation.

Chapter 5

Eventually Guy was offered a job in Cumbria with a big grocers and animal feed shop in Penrith. It was a great job. The new owner was a property developer from London and he wanted the shop to be a Fortnum and Masons. It was Guy's job to make that happen. So we sold our house and moved to Cumbria.

The countryside was fabulous and took me back to my childhood in Rumford. It didn't have the mountains of Scotland but it had awesome rolling hills everywhere. I just loved the land like my gypsy ancestors. I rolled about on it.

We moved into a lovely country hotel in a village called Askham 6 miles from Penrith. It was near the Lowther Estate where the Lowther horse trials were held every year. The Royals competed in that. Then we found a house in Clifton also just a few miles from Penrith. It was a gorgeous stone terrace with roses around the door and on the walls. Nobody locked their houses or their cars. There were no police but the locals looked out for each other.

I got a job in Kendal, a gorgeous town just over the Shap Fells from Clifton, working for a publishing company which produced a magazine for the catering trade in house on the first Apple Macs. I would go round the prospective clients selling advertising space and then designing their ads on the Apple. My years of advertising experience made it very easy for me and I loved the job.

Scarlett was one and a half and we employed a farmer's daughter called Net to be her nanny. She was a healthy outdoors girl and Scarlett was permanently outside in the fresh air. Net would put her on a wee seat on the back of her bike and take her all round the country roads. We would see her wee head above the hedges on the country roads. It was lovely.

Mum and Dad came to visit a lot. It was only 2 hours away from Glasgow and they loved the Cumbrian countryside. Loads of our friends came too so we permanently had a full house. It was a great place for a holiday.

We would go to the Common Riding in Langhom in the Borders not far from us and meet up with the family. We'd been going there every year the last Friday in July for as long as I could remember. All the gypsy ancestors came from there and we would visit their graves in Bentpath and Eskdalemuir.

Every June my Dad and my Uncle Russell would come to Clifton and sneak off to the Appleby Horse Fair. They never took us with them and I always wondered why. I've found out later that it was dangerous for women. The wild gypsies ride bareback and reckless at the fair.

It was all so idyllic but Guy's job was done and so we moved back to Glasgow.

I loved my time in Cumbria but it was great to be back with the family. I quickly got a job at Nationwide Estate Agents as Marketing Manager for Scotland. They gave me a 1% mortgage so we were able to buy a lovely wee terraced house in Burnfield Drive Giffnock. We had some very happy years there. Aimee was born in 1990 so our family was complete.

Guy was working as chef for a restaurant in the West End. He always was a great cook. His Mum had taught him well and he was a natural foodie with a love of all foods. It was there that he got headhunted by a film company and they offered him a job catering for a film. There was big money in this and he was very successful.

We had nanny troubles and two that didn't work out so Scarlett at age 4 insisted she would choose the next nanny. We had two with no teeth then one day we came home from school and Maureen was at the door early for her interview. Our two dogs took to her right away and Scarlett instantly loved her bubbly personality. She had chosen our new nanny and Maureen was with us for years. She was so kind, funny and just adored kids. We had a German cleaner called Mrs Smith who was very stroppy. She thought it was her job to do our washing but Maureen thought it was hers to do the kids since she was the nanny. There were a few arguments but Maureen said she was happy to do the housework too so we let the cleaner go. Maureen was a godsend.

I had done Scotland for Nationwide so they sent me to do my marketing strategy in Newcastle and then Cumbria. It was too much travelling away from my kids and I really missed them. Guy was making loads of money so I decided to leave Nationwide and be with my husband and the children more.

Chapter 6

Guy was doing great doing lots of films and tv working with loads of famous actors like Liam Neeson and Billy Connolly so we could afford to move to a bigger house with our family. We moved to a beautiful bungalow West Winds Thorntonhall in the country. I was back in my favourite countryside. Walking the dogs along the beautiful country roads looking at the sheep. I love sheep. My Dad's cousin Tommy from Eskdalemuir was the guy who took the sheep to auction in a big truck so the sheep are in my genes. I loved chopping the logs for the fire and my Uncle Russell (a great and very funny guy) loved it more than me. It took him back to every summer with his grandparents in Langholm when he was a child. He insisted on doing the chopping whenever he came to visit. He said it was man's work but I'm a toyboy.

Me at Thorntonhall

Langholm

Maureen was the nanny from Heaven and I wanted to keep her so I decided to do part time freelance marketing from our attic. It meant I could come down and see the kids all the time while working and I had loads of time off. I had worked with several housebuilder clients who used Nationwide to sell their properties. I had done all their ads so they were happy to let me continue that. I had some good clients including Ogilvie Homes in Stirling and lots of builders in Ayrshire. I designed their ads on my Apple Mac and printed them on bromide and took them to the newspapers. I made the most money I had ever made in my working life doing that and I still got to spend loads of time with my precious girls.

The house had huge rooms and was perfect for parties. We had a big round table and a grand piano in the living room. Our friends would bring all their kids and Maureen would look after them all. She was like the pied piper they all followed her around. She would arrive with a huge bag of videos and games for them and keep them amused in the playroom and bedrooms while we partied. Then she would put them all to bed.

Mum and Dad never missed a party they were both big party animals and they loved all our family and friends. Mum never drank all her life. She didn't like the taste but Dad loved a few drinks. He would get drunk but you would never know it. He would sit there having extremely interesting conversations with everyone and not appear at all pissed. It was only when he got up to go that his legs would be like jelly. Mum at 5 foot two, and him at 6 foot, would help him down the driveway and drive him home.

We had lots of parties with Guy's actor friends. Actors are great they can all sing and dance so Guy would do the amazing food and they would all be in the kitchen watching him hanging out the fresh pasta to dry. My job was drinks and entertainment so I kept them topped us then I would play Buddy Holly and they would all sing amazingly well. Two of them could play the piano. We all had such fun.

One Christmas we decided to have the whole of my family and Guy's. Graeme and his family came all the way from Cornwall. We hired tables and the lounge became a restaurant with white tablecloths. Guy went to his fav Italian deli in Edinburgh called Valvona Crolla and bought lots of beautiful crystal glasses, wine glasses of all sizes, champagne flutes which looked great on the tables. He even got Grappa glasses because he knew Graeme liked a Grappa. He brought his commercial kitchen (a converted black single decker bus all black with green and red Real Food for Reel People on it) to the garden and did all the cooking out there so there was no mess in the house and the kitchen coped easily with the big numbers .

Boxing Day Graeme wanted to go to Fort William to see his Mum my Auntie Margaret. She ran a hotel up there for years. We decided to go to too. Fort William is a beautiful drive through Glencoe and it had snowed. They clear all the roads instantly but the snow on the mountains of Glencoe is awesome. When we came back Maureen had done all the dishes, cleaned the kitchen and the house was immaculate. What a wonderful woman.

Guy decided that we could work together, have two kitchens and do film and tv catering for two jobs at a time making double the money and it was amazing money we made. The worse the film the more money we made because the filming would run over all the time and they needed more food. My freelance marketing came to an end too. Ogilvie Homes wanted me to do their whole group and it was a big company and also all their PR as well as advertising. This would have meant me subcontracting to other companies and I didn't want to do that. I preferred working on my own so I said no and folded the company. My best job was Trainspotting and my second claim to fame in my life. Trainspotting went to the Cannes Film Festival and I was on the credits with my name in lights. Caterers don't go on TV programmes just films

Dad retired at 58 and bought himself The Readers Digest Book of DIY. It was a massive book. He did all sorts of work about his house in Lynton Avenue. He had a shed which was immaculate he was so OCD. He had all his tools hanging on the walls on hooks and units on the walls with little drawers full of all different sizes of screws and nails. It was so neat and tidy. He had a sink in there for washing his hands and his cassette tape player for his constant jazz. It was his pride and joy. He was so happy in there. He built a wood and metal spiral staircase in his house up to the attic which was his office. He would do his Christmas card list on the first Amstrad computer with one finger. He was mad about jigsaws and he did a 15 foot one of Glencoe. It was on the wall of his office.

Lynton Avenue

There was plenty of work for him to do at West Winds. He used to turn up unannounced. He liked to just drop in on the spur of the moment. He would put up shelves and it was hilarious because he would be drilling holes but he couldn't bear the mess so I would have to stand under him with the nozzle of the hoover against the hole he was drilling so all the bits went down the hoover and didn't make a mess on the floor. I always had his Famous Grouse for him for after he finished a job.

It was in Thorntonhall round the kitchen table that Dad told us he had a shadow on his lung. He'd been coughing up blood and they did an xray and found the lung cancer. He'd always smoked really strong cigarettes Capstan Full Strength, Senior Service and Gitanes and Galois in France. He also smoked his pipe. The devastation we all felt was awful. He was the hub of our family. How were we all going to cope without him. He was only 68. Also my much loved by all of us Uncle Russell died that year from bowel cancer. We were all desperately sad to lose him.

Dad at 68

Dad got treatment. They operated and removed part of his lung. Then he got radiotherapy and chemotherapy. He would go overnight for the chemo at Rosshall private hospital. He made me sneak in the whisky in his overnight bag and he would drink one during the treatment. The nurse said hope your enjoying your apple juice Mr Young. Very funny but his GP had told him a wee whisky was relaxing for the breathlessness you get from lung cancer.

Chapter 7

It's 1995 and my girls are 9 and 5. I'm working on an amazing BBC drama with Ken Stott about a fishfarm on Loch Fyne. We are staying in Tarbert Loch Fyne in the Tarbert Hotel. It's a gorgeous part of Scotland a lovely town with a harbour where a lot of top class boats moored and came in to enjoy the town. The people in the hotel are so friendly and kind. We quickly made friends with Frances and Tottie. The fishfarm is Lochside near Seal Island. Campbeltown is along the scenic road with breakers over the rocks. They did a lot of the filming in Campbeltown, Mull of Kintyre and Southend Beach. A very long beach with white sands and views of Northern Island 12 miles away.

Me and my girls

There was a grapevine in the town so if we needed a dishwasher someone would be waiting outside the hotel at 6 in the morning ready to help us. The milk and rolls men found us wherever we were without us telling them. It's a fishing town so we bought our fish straight from the boats.

My head chef Izzy is from Shetland and she swims with the seals there. After she'd finished lunch she would go swimming at Seal Island. One night in the bar after work she still had her wet swimsuit on. She went upstairs to change for dinner and a lovely wee retired fisherman sat down beside us on her seat. The bar staff had instructions from his wife to send him home if he'd had too much to drink. Anyway he had sat on Izzy's seat so his trousers were all wet and then he went home. The wife called the bar immediately and was shouting at the staff for not sending her husband home before he had wet himself!

Another night we were on a stone terrace outside the Victoria Hotel and I lost my balance and was falling backwards when the big guy from Castlemilk Glasgow with the bad scar on his face from Braveheart leapt across the table and caught me. I could have been seriously injured or even died if my head had hit the stone.

Then I did a job in Sheffield. I loved Sheffield it was a beautiful city with hills all around it. The people were like Glasweigians so friendly and kind. At the fruit and fish markets they couldn't have been more obliging. Rushing to give me everything I needed and if they didn't have anything they would get it for me the same day and deliver it to the truck. We were staying in a luxurious hotel. It was a film about Sheffield United Football Club with Sean Bean and Emily Lloyd. Emily was throwing tantrums galore and refused to do the love scenes. The director had to bring in her mother and father to try and calm her down. She got drunk every night and left clothes strewn in the bar. The porters would fight over who was taking up her breakfast because she was usually naked.

One night there was a huge commotion in the hotel. The Director of Photography and gone to the Producers room with a sawn off shotgun to argue over money. There were police helicopters circling the hotel probably making a huge noise. I've always slept very soundly so I didn't hear a thing. One night Billy Connolly came to visit the cast and crewe. He was in the area. I had a wee chat with him. We are both from Glasgow. I love Billy. I have never missed a gig and I have all his dvds and books.

I was in Manchester on another great job when my Mum called me to tell me Dad had died. He didn't die from the lung cancer. He was watching Tomorrow's World one night and they featured experimental treatment for lung cancer using a laser. Dad spoke to his wonderful GP Dr Kerr who visited him all the time to bring his oxygen see how he was. Dr Kerr found a consultant working on this treatment at Gartnavel Hospital in Great Western Road. Dad had the laser down his throat and it burned off the cancer. He felt great the cancer was gone and he could breathe and eat. He took Mum to One Devonshire Gardens a fine food restaurant next to the hospital. The next day Mum went to see him and he was sitting in an armchair beside the bed dead relaxed and happy watching English football. She went to get him a coffee but when she came back he was dead. The laser had burnt the wound from the operation on his lung and he bled to death. It was a very quick death and he didn't suffer. The lovely consultant wrote to Mum afterwards and said it was a blessing he didn't reach the end stages of lung cancer. They were horrific and he died fighting which made my Dad happy. He loved a fight.

I came back to Glasgow from Manchester and cried and cried rolling about my floor listening to his favourite jazz at full blast. I had to hold it together for my kids during the day but at night I was in bits. It took me seven years to get over the grief. He was such a loving, wonderful man and I was lost without him. Mum paid for me to go to The Priory for grief therapy which helped a lot.

I've thought about him every day for 29 years and I feel him a lot so that helps to know he is happily in Heaven. His funeral was beautiful. He had given us instructions for his funeral when he was 40 round the dinner table. No matter what we were doing when we were growing up Dad always insisted we all sat down for dinner as a family. He told us he wanted no religion at his funeral and he had made a cassette tape of his favourite jolly jazz. His favourite was Louis Armstrong Wonderful World but he knew it would make us all cry. I kept that wee tape for 31 years and for the funeral we got it transferred to cd. We found the only humanist in Scotland at that time from Kilmarnock.

I returned to Manchester after his funeral and I was staying at the Princes Hotel a beautiful hotel in the centre of Manchester. I had a lovely room with a terrace outside the door and a clock tower. I put lots of family pictures of us all and my Dad on the wall above my bed and in the bathroom. It was comforting to remember him. He had such a happy life.

That same year Guy and I decided to separate. We were working apart for so long that we had drifted apart. It was mutual and amicable. The girls were obviously upset at first but they soon realised they were seeing lots of their of Dad as aways. He took them lovely holidays and he bought them ponies which kept them off the streets when they were teenagers. They spent all their spare time with their ponies.

I decided to move into an executive flat so I might meet some hunky business guys. We were right beside Busby station for their commute into work. It was called Glenville Gate. A lovely apartment with a balcony, 3 bedrooms so one for me, Scarlett and one for Aimee. My bedroom had an ensuite and the main bathroom had a jacuzzi. What fun all the kids had with masses of bubbles in the jacuzzi. Unfortunately the residents were mainly retired couples no business men for me to meet except one professional footballer in the block next door to us. I hit it off with him and we had a few dates. He was gorgeous and very fit but there were no sparks so he became just a friend. The oldies were mostly lovely and would invite me in for tea and scones, sometimes a wee sherry and lots of chat. There was one very nosey neighbour Peter on the ground floor who would always come to his door when I was going in and out of the building just to have a nose at me. He never said anything to me. He just looked. It was very irritating. He could at least have said hello where are you off to today but he didn't. The footballer played for Kilmarnock but he then took a job with an English football team and was moving there so he gave me all the contents of his freezer for the kids. Peter was dying to know what was in the bags when he watched us from his open door.

We were deliberately a short walk to Busby Equitation Centre where the girls had their ponies. Scarlett had a lovely bay called Stanley and Aimee had a wee shaggy sandy coloured pony called Spice. They were both gorgeous. Scarlett would ride Stanley down to the flat's car park to come and see me. You should have seen Peter's face then. It was a picture of horror. There was a big horse in his car park that could have touched his car!

Tona and me

He was such a happy person. He loved to sing and he had a great voice. He would be chatting to his friends in the pub and he would just burst into Frank Sinatra. The friends and me all thought he was hilarious. He was always the life and soul of the party and he had loads of friends. Everyone loved Tona.

He had a gorgeous wee flat in Shawlands and we had many great nights there. We both loved Gilbert O'Sullivan and we would dance to him and sing along. We knew all the words.

After my Dad died my Mum didn't want to go back to the South of France. We'd had so many years of wonderful holidays there with Dad she couldn't bear the happy memories when she had lost him. I went just after he died. I thought the happy memories would help with my grief but they made me too sad. I could see him waving at me from the balcony of the lovely flat they had stayed in many times in Juan Les Pins opposite the sea and the amazing private beaches. I came home swiftly. After that family holidays

The first thing I thought is I've met the man with the gold car that Gypsy Rose Lee had told me at the Langholm Fair when I was 14. I was there with my Dad and Uncle Russell. I didn't want to go in. I was scared of gypsies but my Dad persuaded me and I always did what I was told by Dad. He told me I was surrounded by pens and pencils. As a child I preferred stationery shops to toy shops and I have worked in offices for 50 years. He also said I was going to meet a man with a gold car. Also Golfs are my all time favourite car. I love Volkswagens I've had them all my driving life. Tona was also tall, dark and very handsome just like my Granny had predicted in my tea leaves when I was a child.

In the morning we sat at the top of my steps looking out to my fabulous garden drinking coffee and chatting for hours. Then started a whirlwind romance. Tony was permanently snogging me. He love snogging and giving me big bear hugs just like my Dad. The snogging made me feel like I was in my 20s and I was in my 40s. I got massive butterflies in my tummy every time I went to meet him. Tona wasn't just incredibly good looking. He was funny and so interesting. I could talk to him for hours. He'd had a fabulous life. His working life had started off with him owning a jeans factory just as jeans were becoming the fashion in the 70s. He made them himself with a sewing machine and sold them to all the good clothes shops. He went to fashion shows in London and Paris with all the guys from the clothes shops that he sold his jeans to. He made a lot of money and bought a beautiful bungalow in Giffnock. He got out of that just before the recession when all the clothes shops closed.

He did lots of different things and was always successful. When I met him he had a busy sandwich shop in Bath Street then he opened a lovely café opposite Queens Street Station at George Square.

Chapter 8

So I met the Love of my Life Tona at the Redhurst Hotel. His Granny said he was a wee Tona when he was born because he was sallow skinned and dark. I think it's a Scottish word. His real name was Thomas but I called him Tomaso because he looked Italian and I love Italy. The bar was packed and I was there with my best and lifelong friend Audrey. We knew Tona from the crowd from way back. Our kids were in the same class at primary school. That night he was with a good looking guy wearing shorts and flip flops. We called Tona over and asked him if his friend was single for me. He said 'No but I am' and gave me the biggest snog. The whole bar was staring at us and his large group of friends had their mouths open. We rushed out of the bar and went in his gold Golf to The Eglinton Arms in Eaglesham. A lovely hotel in an very pretty village just up the road.

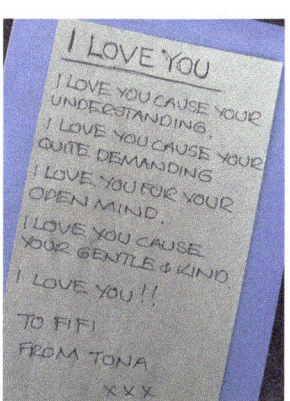

Tona's valentine card

Me in the French Alps

Mum and me at the Colosseum

across the cul de sac was my babysitter and the kids loved her. We spent 15 lovely years there.

I did my last job for the film catering company. It was a Danish commercial for Daz on a beach in Sutherland. Way up north in Scotland with turquoise lochs, the sea and white sandy beaches but it took forever to get there. We had to stop over for the night in Fort William and stay in my Auntie Margaret's hotel. Then we went all the way up the amazing Loch Ness. We didn't see the monster. We stopped at a spectacular hotel. There were wee guys wandering about the grounds in plus fours with big sticks. Deer stalkers. I didn't know they did that anymore. The big guy who owned the hotel was lovely and gay. It was a beautiful hotel and he had flowers everywhere.

The guys in the ad were wearing tartan kilts which turned into white kilts when they washed them with Daz. Hilarious. I stayed in a beautiful blue room in the hotel. Blue is my lifelong favourite colour.

There were masses of heathers everywhere up on the rocks overlooking the sea. I climbed up there and rolled in the heather in my element. A regular boat trip would take people to a massive waterfall that was only visible by sea. It's on my bucket list to go back there some day and see that waterfall.

Anyway I spent most of my time sitting on the kitchen counter looking out and I so missed a garden and lying on the grass. I was such a country girl at heart so we didn't stay at Glenville gate for long. I moved us to a big semi in Clarkston so the girls could go to Williamwood School, the best school in the area. We were on the corner so the garden was huge and on two levels so dead interesting. There was a stone step down from one bit of the garden to the next bit round the corner. We had an apple tree, two plum trees yellow and red and I had a huge area where I grew all our own vegetables. The garden was amazing. I had tomato plants in the glass porch at the top of the back stairs. They grew to ceiling height then across the roof like vines. I had a table and 2 chairs in there and I called it my treehouse because it was up beside the yellow plum tree and the birds in the tree were at eye level. I had always wanted a tree house. I had always loved trees.

The basement was the size of the house and I had my utility down there. I made the big room into a den for the kids and their friends. Just like Mum and Dad had done for us growing up. They decorated it with their drawings of pink Playboy bunnies on black walls. It was great and everyone flocked there. They had great parties with me in the main house checking on them regularly to make sure they weren't doing anything wrong. We had a neighbour we called the witch. She was a horrible woman. Her husband was permanently in his garage pottering probably to escape her. Every time the girls had a party she called the police. What a waste of police time when they could be catching criminals. I answered the door to them and they realised I was in and policing the party so they apologised for bothering me but they had to follow through a complaint from the witch next door. The rest of the neighbours were lovely. A gorgeous girl were in Mallorca for many years. We stayed in hotels with kids clubs and shows at night with the kids dancing to the Macarena and other great songs and dances. Great holidays for us and the kids. When she was 80 my Mum took the whole family on a cruise on the Queen Mary 2. We had her favourite lobster thermadore for her birthday night in the awesome glass and mirrored restaurant. It was our first cruise and it was amazing. She ship was huge and there were jazz bars with smoking areas. My Dad would have loved it. The girls sat on bar stools in the cocktail bar too. Dad loved a bar stool. We sailed round the Caribbean stopping at islands we had never been to before then we sailed up the East coast of the US to New York where we had 4 great nights. Our first visit to New York but it won't be the last for me. I loved the buzz and natural adrenalin you get from that city.

Aboard the Queen Mary 2

Queen Mary 2

We cruised all Mum's 80s. She couldn't get enough of cruises. We progressed to suites with butlers who brought you breakfast on the balconies as we passed Cuba and Jamaica. We had adjoining suites with my girls and they would open the balconies to give us a huge long one. When she reached wheelchair stage in her late 80s it was perfect on a cruise. There were big lifts and wide corridors perfect for wheelchairs and there were plenty of them. Our favourite were Celebrity Cruises which were ultra modern ships. There was music everywhere and the entertainment was always great.

Cruising

Me and Mum at Kirsty's wedding

Tona in France

Then I decided I was ready for Juan Les Pins. It took 7 long years but I had eventually got over my Dad's death so I took Tona. I knew he would love this amazing party town. He loved the sun, gorgeous beaches and swimming in the clear blue Med. I was right he loved it. We went to Mum and Dad's favourite beach with yellow and white mattresses on the sunbeds. The beach restaurants were the best restaurants in town so we always had lunch there. The beach was across the road from La Pinede, a gorgeous park of tall fir trees where the wee old men played boules. Mum used to take my girls there in the pram to get them out of the sun and into the shade of the park. They had some fabulous concerts there with the huge stage erected in front of the beach and the audience in La Pinede. I remember Pink Floyd because Dad got talking to them at the beach bar before the gig. He came home to our flat and said he had been speaking to a pink band. We all laughed. The man and his wife who owned the beach had been there since I went with Mum and Dad. He was even wearing the same clothes. Faded blue baggy jeans and a white cheesecloth shirt. I told him in French I used to come to their beach many years before with my parents and we had always loved his beach.

At night Tona did his John Trevolta in Saturday Night Fever. Getting all dressed up for a night on the town and prancing about looking at his gorgeous self in the big mirror in our apartment. We went to Cannes by train and Mougins a beautiful village of stone buildings and cobbled streets in the mountains above Cannes with artists painting on the streets. All the trainee chefs from the nearby famous French cookery school worked in the restaurants there so the food was phenomenal. Another train the opposite way to Monte Carlo for the day. Just like we had done as a family there. We had the best time.

For the last 10 years Tona had to care for his brother Ian who was deaf and disabled and couldn't look after himself anymore. His parents had left him their family home because they knew he would never be able to work and buy his own home. So Tona moved in to look after him. He was more or less housebound but I used to go and visit them often. I loved Ian he was a big cuddly jolly person despite his disabilities and I had a good ear and could understand what he was saying. Tona and I kept in touch by phone and text and we had lunches often.

Sadly he died young last year at just 64. He had cancer in the spine and in his lung. He had been calling the doctor because he was in constant pain but they would only give him phone appointments. It was his brother's carer who saw him in agonising pain and told him to go to A+E. They instantly transferred him to the Beatson cancer hospital where he died just 10 days later. I went to see him there just before he died and he was eating his dinner, looking good and chatting away. The last words he said to me were 'You look great hen. When I get out of here we'll go for a wee lunch'. He died two days later. I got a garbled text from the massive doses of morphine they were giving him for the pain. I've kept the text and I have lovely pictures of him and us and the Valentine card he gave me on a post it note in frames beside my bed. I kiss them every night.

Chapter 9

Scarlett went to agricultural college near Edinburgh to study horse management. She met lots of farmers, farriers and horsey people, many of them from Arran. She would go to Arran often to see her new friends. She loved it there. It's a beautiful island. Stu was one of the crowd she got in with on the island. She found him a lovely guy and they became good friends.

A while later they started chatting to each other regularly on the phone and text then they arranged to meet up. It was love at first sight for both of them and it wasn't long before Scarlett moved to Arran and they lived in his beautiful white farmhouse in Kilmory. He's a sheep farmer and he also has cows. Scarlett took her horse Oyster there who thoroughly enjoys the freedom and the lovely fields on the farm. She has a friend's horse Black Beauty to keep her company. They also have two gorgeous sheepdogs who live in the barn.

Stu is a beautiful person inside and out. He is so big and strong. He's 6 foot 5 and Scarlett is small like her Gran so she comes up to his waist. Just like my Mum and Dad. He's so kind, loving, funny and fun loving. There is a lot of laughter in their house just like when I was growing up. He's also fantastic at DIY so he does up their house. He can even do electrics. He got that at college and he is a trained mechanic. He repairs all his and his family's tractors and farm equipment

His proposal was very romantic on one knee on their winding pebbled driveway with sheep in the fields next to it and views of the sea and Ailsa Craig. A gorgeous uninhabited island off the coast of Ayrshire. There are just beautiful birds there.

They were getting married 3 years ago but they decided to have their family first. They have two gorgeous girls Lottie 2 and Zoe 6 months. I adore my 2 grandaughters and they love me loads too. The wedding is next year in the barn on their farm. It will be fabulous with the barn all decorated with plants from the farm and fairy lights everywhere. I can't wait.

Scarlett Stu and Lottie

Aimee met Kyle at school when she was 14. They were in the same class. Aimee wasn't doing well at Williamwood. She was in a big class and struggling a bit. The teacher didn't have time to help her. So we moved her to a private school called Belmont in Newton Mearns. That's where she became great friends with Kyle. She used to take him to visit her Gran and they went out with their classmates to pubs and clubs in Glasgow. Kyle is very handsome. Tall and sallow skinned with tousled light brown hair so lots of the girls fancied him. To get rid of them in the clubs he would kiss Aimee and pretend she was his girlfriend and they would back off.

One day we came home from school and there was a bouquet of flowers on the doorstep with a card. The card simply said 'Be mine' love Kyle. He wanted to be more than friends. Aimee wasn't sure at first they were such good friends she thought that would be spoiled but she soon got over that and they became inseparable. They still did all the same stuff they had done when they were friends.

Their engagement was very romantic too. It was Christmas Day and Kyle had little presents all they way up the tree for Aimee. They always did lovely things for each other at Christmas. When she got to the top of the tree there was a beautiful red gold ring in the box. He said marry me on one knee at the bottom of their beautiful tree.

Their wedding was magical. It was a glorious sunny day in September in Kinkell Byre in St Andrews on the East coast beside the sea. The company supplied all the fairy lights on the walls and hanging from the ceiling but the rest of the decoration was up to you. Aimee and Kyle were in their element designing the room for their wedding. They had beautiful wooden tables and chairs. Place names made out of thin wood, gorgeous glassware and little bouquets of Scottish heather on all the tables. The whole room was full of brightly coloured flowers the same as the bride and bridesmaids. All handpicked by Aimee. The food came in Land Rovers and one person was designated from each table to put on a pinny, collect the food and distribute it to the table. Ian Robertson an actor friend of Guy's did Tam O'Shanter by heart while acting it out amongst the tables.

Their honeymoon was in South Africa on safari for a couple of days, then Capetown swimming with the sharks and penguin beach and then the wine region. Aimee loves Africa. She volunteered in an orphanage in Ghana and did her placement for her midwifery degree at a hospital in Tanzania.

They've been married for 8 years this year and they have two wonderful children. Alfie 6 and now at school and Mila 4. I adore my clever, funny and gorgeous grandkids.

Chapter 10

So I spoke to Tona at length through a psychic last week. She said I've got your husband here and he passed very quickly. I said I don't have a husband but I have a partner who died in 10 days. Every card she turned over was my husband again. It happened 6 times. Eventually she said he is saying he is your husband and he wishes he'd married me way back when we met. That was 29 years ago so I could have been married to the love of my life for all that time.

I would happily have lived with Tona in my house with his brother in my spare room. I loved Ian and I would have learned sign language so I could speak to him properly. Anyway he told the psychic his birthday is 10th July and he hoped I would remember him then. How could I forget his birthday. I have already planned to listen to our favourite Gilbert O'Sullivan and dance and sing along to it like we used to do often.

How wonderful to be dying and know that I am going to our wedding in Heaven with all my family and friends one day.

I felt Mum the minute she died just like Dad. Massive goosebumps and I knew it was her because I couldn't stop thinking about her and the wonderful 96 years we had had together. She is with me all the time watching over me. I know Dad would be letting her spend all this time with me because he has had me for 29 years and that's the kind man that he is and he adores us all.

Last month I decided to stop my wine drinking for my 70s. I had one sleepless night but Mum was right by my side helping me along. She never drank anything in her whole life. She didn't like the taste of alcohol. The day before I stopped dead I had two drinks and the wine tasted awful. I have a great wine palette and I only buy the good stuff but Mum had made it taste so bad.

She has told me that she is my wee dog Peppa. She has done reincarnation which she has said is very difficult for a spirit to do. You have to be a very powerful spirit to do it. Mum is and so is Dad. He was a tall dark handsome sheepdog I had 23 years ago called Sweep. They've told me I'm a very powerful medium too. I just need to do meditation then I will hear all the spirits clearly. I am going to a Buddhist monastery in Eskdalemuir in the Scottish Borders next month to learn meditation.

Sweep

Samye Ling Tibetan Buddhist Monastery

Peppa is very small but beautiful, loving and feisty just like my Mum. On my sleepless night that little dog stuck to me like glue. When I went upstairs to try and sleep she came up with me. Then when I came down to watch tv because I couldn't sleep Peppa came too. Outside to the garden for a cigarette and she was there. This went on for the whole night and it was Mum helping me through that night. I love having my Mum beside me all the time.

Peppa

Birds, butterflies and feathers are spirits. While writing this book I have had so many Magpies on my garden fence. That tall dark handsome bird is my Dad. Then a Magpie and a Crow. That's my Dad and my Uncle Russell who are always together with their whiskies. They look identical only Russell is a smaller version of my Dad. One day last week there were two Crows in the lovely Linn Park with my dog. Dad and Uncle Russell the gypsies love the land and walking amongst the trees like me. My Mum is a Robin. Small and gorgeous. I see them in the woods at the park. We don't get many robins in Glasgow so I don't get them at home but Scarlett gets loads on Arran and she knows Mum is watching over her too. There was a Red Admiral butterfly on my bedroom today. I caught it and got it safely out the window. I think it was Tona because I am writing about our wedding today.

Mum and Dad have been a big help to me writing this book. They have been with me every step of the way remembering things that I may have forgotten. I love you both and I can't wait to see you one day.

www.ingramcontent.com/pod-product-compliance
Lightning Source LLC
Chambersburg PA
CBHW071221070526
44584CB00019B/3102